THE KING'S QUESTION

Winner of the
Emily Dickinson First Book Award
from the Poetry Foundation

THE KING'S QUESTION

Poems by
BRIAN CULHANE

Graywolf Press
SAINT PAUL, MINNESOTA

Publication of this volume is made possible in part by a grant provided by the Minnesota State Arts Board, through an appropriation by the Minnesota State Legislature; a grant from the Wells Fargo Foundation Minnesota; and a grant from the National Endowment for the Arts, which believes that a great nation deserves great art. Significant support has also been provided by the Bush Foundation; Target; the McKnight Foundation; and other generous contributions from foundations, corporations, and individuals. To these organizations and individuals we offer our heartfelt thanks.

Winner of the 2007 Emily Dickinson First Book Award established by the Poetry Foundation to recognize an American poet over the age of fifty who has yet to publish a first book.

Published by Graywolf Press
2402 University Avenue, Suite 203
Saint Paul, Minnesota 55114
All rights reserved.

www.graywolfpress.org

Published in the United States of America

ISBN 978-1-55597-511-1

2 4 6 8 9 7 5 3 1
First Graywolf Printing, 2008

Library of Congress Control Number: 2008928256

Cover design: Kyle G. Hunter

Cover art: Fragment of the Stele (grave marker) of a hoplite (foot soldier). The Metropolitan Museum of Art, Fletcher Fund, 1938. (38.11.13) Photograph © 1997 The Metropolitan Museum of Art.

ACKNOWLEDGMENTS

Grateful acknowledgments to the editors of the following periodicals, where poems in this book first appeared, sometimes in different versions:

Alaska Quarterly Review: "This Winter" and "Angelus Novus"

Antaeus: "History of the Mediterranean"

Chelsea Review: "Glossarium"

Columbia Magazine: "The Western Intellectual Tradition"

The Hudson Review: "For One Who First Showed Me Scipio's Dream," "Hexameter," "The King's Question," "Another Europe," and "Harrow in Field"

The New Criterion: "Paradigm"

The New Republic: "Monument"

The Paris Review: "Knowing Greek," "Chekhov's 'The Student' (April, 1894)," "Error," and "Library"

Shenandoah: "Estrangement in Athens"

Southern Humanities Review: "The Last *Canto*"

I would also like to record my gratitude, which extends well beyond this book's horizon, to Christopher Z. Hobson and Michael Pillinger, whose friendship and literary counsel have sustained me these past three decades.

CONTENTS

SCIPIO'S DREAM
Error 3
Paradigm 4
Library 5
Hexameter 8
History of the Mediterranean 9
Monument 10
Knowing Greek 12
For One Who First Showed Me Scipio's Dream 14
This Winter 16
The King's Question 18

JUST A MOMENT TO MEMORIZE THE PAST
Harrow in Field 23
Another Europe 26
Estrangement in Athens 28
Chekhov's "The Student" (April, 1894) 29
The Last *Canto* 31
The Western Intellectual Tradition 33
Shadow Work 34
Philosophy, Writ Small 36
Angelus Novus 39

BEYOND BOOK'S HORIZON
At Wallace Stevens' Grave 43
For Z. Herbert 46
Posthumous 48
Glossarium 51
Envoi 64

Notes 67

FOR MY WIFE, **VICTORIA,**
  AND MY CHILDREN, **WILL** AND **ELIZA**

There was once an artist
Faithful and hardworking. His workshop,
Together with all he had painted, burned down,
He himself was executed. Nobody has heard of him.
Yet his paintings remain. On the other side of fire.

Czeslaw Milosz

SCIPIO'S DREAM

ERROR

It remains to be seen if I lose my way
In a meadow somewhere beyond today
In a season foretold perhaps, in a future
Whose accent is a footfall on dry leaves
Or the sighing of a sibyl beside a stream
That sharply flows into the cave mouth,
Into undergrowth none walks out of.
That is one story. There are a few others
Illustrated by Doré: the ancient wood
One moment's false step will prove
Permanent and unrecognizably pathless:
The forest known in retrospect as Error,
Whose root lies tangled in wandering.
Once upon a time to fall fully awake
And descend to a height. The journey starts
At the omphalos lip, the navel ring
Where the blackened stone circle charms
The wayward into mounting slowly down
Granite steps, past the silenced Geryon,
Deeper and deeper yet, until one thrust
And there's starlight, hearing a highway's
Whine, a factory whistle, a far siren
Calling you out of brambles and stone
Only to find the hillside started from:
Your fabled self, lying there error prone.

PARADIGM

Cool pressure of prescience, this snow
Against the familiar, gritty pavement
Of New York. A piano plays rapidly
And in ignorance: accumulations
Deepening throughout the night.
What solo casts its spell on the moon?
Only scales, left hand after right,
As steady as this snow, ascent
And descent, the way lovers talk
To themselves at night, higher, lower,
Always searching for the opposing touch,
The steady snow, these lucent attitudes,
Crystallizations at some further remove.

LIBRARY

Paulatim lachrymas rerum experentia tersit.
Petrarch

Father's books lying on the living-room floor
Must be divided into threes: art history,
Classical letters and, left from my days here,
Unsteady stacks of quasi-educational lore
That show yellowing *Geographic* scientists
Perennially lost in rain forest mists.
An instant choice will cull some from the rest
So they may become mine—a banausic test.

Prewar light glimmers in the apartment:
A shadowplay that summons an adolescence
Of slammed doors and risible nothings
Hurled at retreating parental backs
—The most telling blows always *sotto voce*—
As I stormed and wept and read in silence.
Now, standing again in silence, I stare
At a word trove given two sons to share.

Some are dated in the first blank page: *1
January 1938* this reads, as if a resolution
Made (and kept?); this ruddy leather edition
States simply *Property of*—with no name given.
I gesture toward the emptiness of gifts
Prematurely bestowed in illness's ruin,
And blow dust off an enfeebled spine,
Filling lungs with belletristic grime.

It's all some forgotten chore from a childhood
The hall mirror charitably declares was good.
Pictures of other libraries fill my head:
Weighty tomes I hauled to girlfriends' walkups,
Barely unpacked before again in boxes;
Or Sophoclean dramas, lost to ancient fires,
Which exist in name only; or that fable
Of an infinitely circular Library of Babel

Borges saw as self-referential: nooks,
Corridors, dead ends, twisting stairwells:
Bibliographic cargo cults and infidels.
In his bed, dreaming of a golden age of looks
And cars, booze and fine clothes, my father snores
And chokes and comes to. . . . Sunlight pours
Into empty bookcases. *Where in hell are they?!*
If memory then corrects, questions stay

And, refracting off walls, gather numb force
As I read a volume plucked at random
Only to start up when hoarse ripples burn
My innermost ear: *Where, where, where?*
Soon my father will awaken to find no air.
One tattered cover shows a boy's ray-gun
Pointed to the sun: the future, that much is clear.
Somewhere where this library can cohere.

Nearly finished, I stumble on Petrarch's *Epistles*
And, apropos of age, find: *In that passing, I shall*
Not seem myself: another brow, other habits, a new form
Of the mind, another voice sounding. . . . Father whistles
Down the hallway for his lackadaisical firstborn.
Little by little, experience wipes dry our tears.
The job's done—leaving me to calculate the years
I withheld my love, and the years I've left to mourn.

HEXAMETER

Hold, memory, a vision out of Greece:
The west wind breathes a ripening breath
As each pear, pendant and golden, brushes
Another, where four tilled acres glisten
Winter and summer: fig, olive, currant,
And the heavy succulent pomegranate
—Sunstruck for the plucker's hand.
All this a stranger sees, palm on lintel,
Sees the stately women of the royal rooms
Murmuring over linen, looms humming;
Sees boys, on pedestals, shine torches
Which fire the eyes of Alkinöos's hounds.

So much of heroism wondrously found
(Like a glinting pebble in a child's hand,
Borne upward to imagination's shallows),
As I'd gaze at snow blanketing West End,
Hearing the story my father burnished
Over a month of nights, so that the voyage
Of the telling faded into the hours lived
Beside that voice—whiskey rough—again
Taking up the exile's lament: *hekatomb,
Distaff, honeyed wine* . . . Some bleary god
Come down from heaven's height, as snow
Descends on elms and, beyond our window,
Odysseus, beggared and unknown, moves
Toward the great bow of gnarled revenge.
Father, I stand beside you now, your right arm!
Pitch pine torches reveal a stranger's son
Holding still-thrumming wood in his hand.

HISTORY OF THE MEDITERRANEAN

Not as Braudel did it, the hegemonies
Of trade and the grand sweep. Nor yet
As those three-walled frescoes studded
With the sweat of innumerable angels.
I mean the gravity of feeling
Whose small wave without acclaim scatters
Redolent sand. Or a cheap hotel lobby:
Widow and widower talking beside a pillar
Of no particular importance
But that their marvelous lives lend.
Luxury bereft of years' weight, no
Chiseled imprimatur, marble freed
From the centurion's implacable shadow.

So, the day's gauntlet thrown, stand
On this Tuscan hill and watch as noon
Ripples the flax of distant homes.
In ahistorical sunlight we murmur,
Repeating the ever-to-be-repeated.
Pull your dress off and find the wind.

MONUMENT

L.B. (1955–1979)

Of that year I remember the soft gauzy
Whitish lump of goat cheese going bad

Like some alchemical disaster turning day
To lead; the Cretan sun so much Minoan

Bull-leapers' somersaulting glory; and you
Looking down the long sluice of months

Toward the metonymy of hospital walls,
Gums dyeing your first Greek hours,

Smearing the hope that brought you here
For one last fling at life. . . . Recovering

From the flight, you pondered my room's
Garish poster of Manhattan's skyline,

Epic in black and white. You caught flaws
In its silhouette only a native could,

Seated before the memory of all you were.
What height had you risked, Lloyd, to come

From the bedridden gloom of Astoria, Queens,
Just to face anachronistic splendor?—you

Whose marrow I'd soon sift though fingers
On a hillside far from any possible future:

Snow's soot on a Catskill lake, after our
Palms patted the silvered seam of earth down.

KNOWING GREEK

for Hazard Adams

Once it seemed possible, those boys
Peeking out of gun slits at the German line
Or on graves detail, wet, miserable,
Oblivious to the dawn's miserable joys.
I hardly know what to say to their faces,
Locked away in secret histories of the war,
The Great one, which was lost, really lost,
By the victors at Versailles. Sure, I could go
To pastured no-man's-land, yet another
In a shambling line of the misinformed,
Staring, too ready to honor landscape.
What have we learned? A teacher's question.
Russell's *Principia Mathematica* proved false,
No doubt, and the decades have never ceased
From accelerating to where I now sit
In the Elgin Room ("De Greeks were Godes!"
Shouted Fuseli at first seeing the marbles),
Contemplating the beauty that brought Byron
To fight for liberty against the Turks
—Broken by marsh fever at Missolonghi,
His valet Fletcher still with him. Shelley,
Legend has it, drowned with a Greek play
Stuck in a pocket. "We are all Greeks," he said.
In Rome, I have walked the piazza where
His friend's deathsheet burned. Keats had no Greek.
He wrote his sonnet to Chapman's Homer
Out of ardor for an epic Englished.
For him, too, breathing and Greek came together,
If only as absence, some swift final pain.

Yes, on to Pi, / When the end loomed nigh
—So newly-dead Liddell to long-dead Scott
On their alphabetical quest, and I
Look again at the forms the good Lord saved
To steal and bury in this London sanctuary.
Athanatos, deathless; *psuche,* soul: engraved
On my mind since ephebe days at City College
Where I copied out my own slim lexicon.
Marathon may be more important than Hastings
"Even as an event in English history,"
But noting the shortness of their upper lips,
Carlyle vexed the painter Watts by claiming
Pheidias's sculpted men lacked cleverness.

Yes. Once it seemed possible, those boys
With their classical educations bursting
Like gods from mud, kissing reddening stones
Still redder under a pockmarked plain.
All those undying souls writing home
As the first mechanized war stole their words,
As *lads* became *men,* and *honour* came to what?
You're never so right as when you're dead,
The marbles seem to say; or with Peleus
To his son, *Always be the champion;* or, with Weil,
Force is any x that makes a thing out of a mortal
—A sudden swarm of centuries gone wrong.
In marmoreal light I raise a chastened hand:
Beauty is truth, a sick youth's equation.
Trenches lie on the surface of my palm.

FOR ONE WHO FIRST SHOWED
ME SCIPIO'S DREAM

Professor Alan S. Fisher, d. 2003

Alan, it is late.
This bar is closing
And all your fine talk
Won't buy us a drink.

No, I haven't forgotten
You are lately dead—
Walking, mid-step, fallen.
So like you to leave

Walking and thinking:
Your fighter's squint
Unable to make out
The final stroke.

Alan, the bar is closing
And I'm for the cold.
It's grown dark,
But you're still laughing,

Quoting: *And that one talent*
Which is death to hide. . . .
I'd laugh with you
But all my money's spent.

Your faded corduroy
Jacket's off the hook.
No more literature tonight.
Not even a last look.

THIS WINTER

Out of the clear winter sky
A phone rings through dreams
Until I swing a hand
Into the element of day
And hear intimations, raw
Weeping, muffled Swedish,
That make me lean over to shake her
Whose name is a bifoliate
Blue flower.

So they search his apartment:
The dishes clean and stacked,
The fridge turned off, work keys
Bunched and labeled.
Beyond: a scraggly woods
Where his father had once found him
Bleeding at both wrists,
Sobbing drunk. Nine years ago.

This time he's not unearthed
Hungry and repentant. Yesterday
New storms covered his tracks:
Footfalls a boy spotted in a copse
Arrowing toward the bay
Where his ship, *Penelope,*
Waits shrouded on blocks.
For luck, his daughter
Has safety-pinned his photo
To the telephone cord. . . .

A week after his disappearance:
Nothing, no body, no trace,
Until, according to reports,
Spring's ramifications when lakes,
Freed of ice, give up their once-
Thrashing souls to billhooks.
Then small flowers, fed by brooks,
May grip the countryside
In a shudder of color, tiny aches
Swelling to a pool of blue
That pulls as it clears
The way loss does and will do.

THE KING'S QUESTION

In memory of Nancy Tow Spiegel

Before he put his important question to an oracle,
Croesus planned to test all the famous soothsayers,
Sending runners half around the world, to Delphi,
Dodona, Amphiarius, Branchidae, and Ammon,
So as to determine the accuracy of their words;
His challenge: not to say anything of his future

But rather what he was doing in his capital, Sardis
(Eating an unlikely meal of lamb and tortoise,
Exactly one hundred days after messengers had set out).
This posed a challenge, then, of far space not of time:
Of seeing past dunes and rock fortresses; of flying,
Freighted, above caravans and seas; of sightedness,

As it were, in the present construed as a darkened room.
Croesus of Lydia sought by this means to gauge
The unplumbed limits of what each oracle knew,
Hesitant to entrust his fate to any unable to divine
Lamb and tortoise stewing in a bronze pot.
When only the Pythia of Apollo at Delphi correctly

Answered from her cleft, her tripod just the lens
For seeing into the royal ego, she put his mind to rest,
But not before speaking in her smoke-stung voice:
I count the grains of sand on the beach and the sea's depth;
I know the speech of the dumb and I hear those without voice.
We know this because those present wrote it down.

Of the King's crucial question, however, there is nothing.
We have no word. The histories are silent.

                            My analyst,
Whose office on Madison was narrow as an anchorite's cave,
Would sit behind me as I stared up at her impassive ceiling,
As the uptown buses slushed all the way to Harlem,
And I would recount, with many hesitations and asides,

The play that I was starring in, whose Acts were as yet
Fluid, though the whole loomed tragically enough.
She would listen, bent over knitting, or occasionally note
Some fact made less random by my tremulous soliloquy.
When much later I heard of her death after long cancer,
I walked across town and stood, in front of her building,

Trying to resurrect those afternoons that became the years
We labored together toward a time without neurosis,
When I might work and raise a family and find peace.
Find, if not happiness exactly, some surcease from pain.
What question had I failed to ask, when the chance was mine?
When she, who knew me so well, could have answered?

Let just one of those quicksilver hours be returned to me,
With my knowledge now of the world, and not a boy's,
With all that I have become a lighted room. One hour
To ask the question that burned, once, in a King's throat:
The question of all questions, the true source and center,
Without which a soul must make do, clap hands and sing.

JUST A MOMENT TO
MEMORIZE THE PAST

HARROW IN FIELD

anonymous oil on panel, c.1600

If geography's what's left when history
Fades to some final erratum stuck
To the foot, scraped off like cowdung
At the door,

Then we have come to the right place,
A field, this field, the smell of earth,
Dawn, and two clownish Dutchmen
(*Clown* from *clod*—

A derivation wholly lost to the midden
Unless centuries are pried back to show
The brown-clotted, briny stuff
That dike's flood

Left as some glomming pestilence
To stick and stick again to plodders
Striking out for godforsaken
Mud-brown flats).

If there's a meaning to their work
We cannot derive it from blotches
Sublimely thrown against sky,
Like dark mud

On lighter mud, and the historian
Is obliged to note the brazen lack
Of individualizing detail:
Men are clods,

Clods making clowns of any man.
This is what the years' receding muck
Has left on pasture, anvil, gate
Dull in sun;

While someone, a bare-armed woman,
No more than a brushstroke's blur,
Leans from a window calling the two
Back—or not—

The sun streaking her cocked head;
While soldiers harrowing geese
Wheel and turn in sodden furrows:
Just out of

Reach they seem, at plowed margins:
Moving, as they are, toward a westerly
Vanishing point whose coordinates
Must be *thence*.

One woman and two oafs known
To us in the clumsy certainty bestowed
By ignorance on time, and what's known
Is soon lost

In unsalvageable earthworks formed
On clod-strewn turf and, farther, down
Into the damp heart of Flemish dawns,
Clod turns *clown*

And so on, through eelgrass, past weirs
(Voices embogged in waterweeds);
Through long nights of peasant uprisings
And wan kings

Mustered on mounds of castlemud,
And the cold, heavy, golden things
Sunk along with the names, the wars
And the biers.

Trenchmud, hillmud, acres of sludge—
We raise our eyes to the horizon's
Faint smudge that asks, *Can you bear
The fresh touch*

Of loam, bear how it works under nails?
The two men clump off in heavy clogs.
Now watch as the girl watches crops fail.
Stand near. Here.

ANOTHER EUROPE

My wife's father sits on a plank bench nodding over a language.
It is the tongue of childhood. It is summer in another country

And in woods other children—a brother, sisters, cousins—
Mimic plaintive birdcalls, deep in a thicket of stratagems:

For they are young and in love with the way daylight descends
Through spruce with a long and distinguished lineage.

My wife's father closes his eyes more tightly to hear the *berceuse*
Of his beloved nurse, but all he can make out is the main gate

Closed fast, while the mutterings of leather-smocked peasants
Fall against the castle and plunge, pricking the moat like rain.

There is a region in the past that summons memory just to
       bruise it.
There wells an inflection known to us in childhood: melodious.

It is frost creaking floorboards. Or storekeepers sweeping.
Or doves brooding long over the indignities of creation.

Were it possible to open some high window onto the bell tower!
For only in homecoming's syllables, back in the cave of dialect,

Can recompense for elsewheres be truly made. And that, barely.
A boy who was a man who was a boy takes giant strides, stirred

By what joy or sorrow? In what century? To him come anthems,
Oaths, fortunes, runes, riddles, fiddle tunes, prayers. To him

The benediction of innocents. A lashed mule. A cat struck lame.
Then the firestorm's thunder as field guns wrinkle the horizon.

A lost sister bends down, saying his name. And far overhead
The guttural song of exile touches the branches to awaken him.

ESTRANGEMENT IN ATHENS

Mount Olympus held nothing for them.
No occasion of theirs could provoke
Magniloquent debate. Nor act require
That attic of gods to come swooping
Onto the field, swaying the battle.
Only the great booming of the ferry
As it shouldered alongside the pier;
Only the waitress counting their
Saucers; it was this April morning
That swung them by their heels.
What was missing was the impersonal,
The fated, a visionary marble address,
The goddess skimming over blue water
To whisper good news, or some stud,
Swan, or bull brimming with light.
Not a wingéd foot. Only Love,
Recently decamped, hovered above
The table, ready to be splendid.
But their ten years' war had ended.

CHEKHOV'S "THE STUDENT" (APRIL, 1894)

For hours now the Last Supper has been over,
And the beating almost over, and morning's cry
Yet to be heard by the workmen in the courtyard
Warming themselves by the hasty fire, and Peter,
Near the agony in the garden, feeling something
Terrible happening, blinking back stale sleep,
Peter turns his face from strangers' stares.
"This man also was with Jesus." Then others
Slowly turning toward him with cold interest,
And his own voice, thick-tongued: "I do not know him."

That the cock crows not then but at the third *No*
Must tell us much about the nature of faith,
How it leans on separations, how it robes simple
Gestures—a hand waving from an open window—
With deferral, as if real knowledge only comes after,
As though Peter could only see what he'd done
Upon going from the high priest's courtyard
And, all alone, weeping bitterly in the dawn.
That much we can understand, but why then
Does Chekhov revisit this known, hard ground

With a half-frozen student who, on his way back
From a failed hunt, thinks how this same chill
Easter wind must have blown in Rurik's age
And scourged the hungry poor in the years
Of Peter the Great and Ivan the Terrible?
Wind, raw wind, hunger, icy needles of rain . . .
The same as then—until, coming on two widows,
A huge, shapeless old woman in a man's overcoat
And her putty-faced daughter washing a kettle,
The student asks if he might share their fire,

Saying, as he does, that St. Peter had on such
A night warmed himself before a fire, on such
A cold, extraordinarily long and terrible night.
Murmuring welcomes, they bring him inside,
And soon he finds himself describing in detail
That part of the gospel which is Peter's betrayal:
". . . thus I imagine it: the garden deathly still
And very dark, and in the silence came
Sounds of muffled sobbing—" Here his account
Breaks off when the absently-smiling Vasilissa

Suddenly weeps, burying her eyes in her apron;
Whereupon her daughter, herself bowed down
By sickness and filth, blushes and turns away.
The student, for all his theology, is speechless.
There's nothing for it now but to step out
With empty game-bag and find his moonlit
Way back home across the ancient marsh.
Only then does he see in the waterlogged
Meadow, well beyond the river's sedges,
Something remarkable: a high-walled garden

Looming green against a background of sand.
Nineteen hundred years crossed in heartbeats!
In that kindled instant all the world's travails
Drop from his shoulders. Just twenty-two,
He has found the very quick of faith.
Gone are hunger, sleet and useless words. Gone!
Ah, we leave him there at century's end,
Before he has returned to his village
—And all that returning would surely mean—
In this, the briefest of the master's stories.

THE LAST *CANTO*

In the garrulous present
Threadbare nouns find
What raiment's left
From forefathers

Who perhaps struck poses
But wrote of frenzy
Out of deepest urgency
Hammering voices

In no dumbfounded age.
Theirs the grace
Of unfaltering
Fealty to the word.

Yet then I picture Pound
Prematurely stilled
By his own tongue
—*Tempus tacendi.*

Did he ever revisit
The barbed floodlit quad
Where bareheaded he'd
Stood in all weather

Mouthing surreal Greek,
Fashioning a rhythm
Out of life's ruin,
That life he would unspeak

Half a lifetime later
Arriving on the tarmac
Of Eisenhower Italy,
Breath caught in the throat?

I heft his burdened book
Only to let it drop
—A stoneweight dropping down
Well's jaggy darkness

That anyhow comes back
In stonecold dialect:
Pisa! A pure echo
Purged of memory.

On my lap his poems'
Esoteric call
Has no words at all
Or just those selfsame ones

Quarried from a rock
—Red and ocher bison
Emblaze the solitude
Of an old draughtsman

Who long hours daubs
In Altamira's shade:
Let those I love try to forgive
What I have made.

THE WESTERN INTELLECTUAL TRADITION

Perhaps begin with Gilgamesh's better half, Enkidu,
From whose nose did fall the worm of death;
Or that psalmist who saw Gilead in the love act,
Two sweating selves making the little death;

But whatever you do begin with the construct *you*—
A tautology Descartes loved teasing to death;
Perhaps start with the monumentality of fact:
A famous thought, a *first*, not so unlike a last breath.

SHADOW WORK

Desk lamp casts a shadow on the page.
I turn to a column of print
And it too goes on.
Shadow work, again.
Turning pages, I enact
The rhythm of years.
Perhaps this book with frayed edges
Partakes in a grand fiction
That begins with an *Oh*
And ends with some eschatology
Yet to be born.
As when a tourist wanders over Athenian rubble
And blocks out roiling traffic,
Hearing, yes, the bray of an ass
In the Stoa's cool colonnade:
The war must be prosecuted until
They are outfought, drummed in the dirt.
But thereupon comes the stench
Of Sicilian quarries
Where one slave, in final extremity,
Considers the histories made of dust
And his own life
Braiding a girl's hair beside the sea.

Work table. Lamp light—
Glow of flames from Lindisfarne:
The sanctuary broken, strawhairs
Ransacking, burning, hacking:
Monks in flight long months
And St. Cuthbert's Book lost

In the sands of the Solway Firth,
Only to be found when Hunred,
Bearer of Cuthbert's coffin,
Saw the missing relic in a vision.

Lamp light; shadow work.
This book absorbs all light.
If only we knew what word to leave on
—But that's not something given.
In any event, when the angel calls
And we rise, choking earth,
It won't help to have the right theory
Or shake your neighbor's hand.
Sunlight will fall like dust
And the pages of the Book
Shall open in memory of
Everything you ever forgot.
The simplest things last.

PHILOSOPHY, WRIT SMALL

After Sebald

The iniquity of oblivion blindly scatters
her poppyseed and when wretchedness
falls upon us one summer's day like snow,
all we wish for is to be forgotten.

Forget oblivion or its blown poppyseed.
Wretchedness falls upon us,
and all we wish is to be scattered like snow.

And because it is so, it befits our philosophy
to be writ small, using the shorthand
and contracted forms of transient Nature,
which alone are a reflection of eternity.

Contrary to popular belief, it is not difficult
to burn a human body: a piece of an old boat bottom
burnt Pompey, and the King of Castile burnt
large numbers of Saracens with next to no fuel,
the fire being seen far and wide.

Here are curiosities: the circumcision knives
of Joshua, the ring which belonged to the mistress
of Propertius, an ape of agate, a grasshopper,
three-hundred golden bees, a blue opal,
silver belt buckles and clasps, iron pins, brass plates
and brazen nippers to pull away hair,
and a brass jew's-harp that last sounded
on the crossing of the black water.

Here the ape of agate, here the knife of Joshua,
here the silver clasps and rings and pins;
here a poppyseed beside an old boat bottom, torched.

Contrary to popular belief, these curiosities
are reflections of an eternity of knives, of rings,
of brazen nippers and, far off, the fires seen

from a Roman urn

on the horizon, where once the Saracens
danced to the jew's-harp in the days of Propertius,
the time of our Nature, now writ small.

Here are our curiosities
The most marvelous item, from a Roman urn
preserved by Cardinal Farnese, is a drinking glass,
so bright it might have been newly blown.

This is our philosophy of inequity,
whose tune the jew's-harp plays in the hours
of Propitious; here the agate ape mouths

the poppyseed

most marvelous

Oblivion becomes the final fruit of all certainties
and what remains

in the urns is examined closely: the ash,
the loose teeth, some long roots of quitch,
or dog's grass wreathed about the bones,
and the coin intended for the Elysian ferryman.

    Flame fills the new-blown drinking glass.
    Drifting toward the smoking shore,
    our ferryman, wreathed with golden bees,
    points out ash, teeth, bones: a mound
    of dog's grass

Wretchedness falls upon us

    and Pompey himself, standing there
    rooted like quitch, though soon forgotten
    in sudden marvelous snow.

ANGELUS NOVUS

Back from the catastrophe of the paradisal past:
This steady crescendo of wind. This continuous wind.

The act of knowing is a single gesture: present, past,
Future, merely floating logs on either side of a wind-

Cleft river, as Wittgenstein says. Metaphor for past
Events slipping by the *Blue Book*'s shore. "Wind-

Cleft" too poetic for his German; his flowing past
Northern, solitary, laconic. Floes. A chastening wind.

Or take that other man, Walter Benjamin, whose past
One rainy night in 1940 became a suicide's breathless wind,

Cleaving time into two disparate streams, where past
And aggrieved future flow unevenly onward and no wind

Relieves his mind of a tortured backward look: past,
A conspicuous chain of events, though the stale wind

Of lips gone blue suggests the apothegm's purity is past
Helping; the grand amalgamating fugues of reason, wind

From a boxcar. Wittgenstein was fond of spending his past
In a Norwegian hut where waves scissor before wind.

He'd write thoughts on slips of paper. Like the past,
They accumulated in a shoebox. Like Klee's angel facing wind,

He watched them drift. Call them "things from the past."
Sometimes say, "from the Past." Such subtlety is lost in wind.

A moment divided Benjamin from the now, from underscoring *past*
In his notebook (itself fluttering in the Vichy wind),

From sailing to Palestine. Just a moment to memorize the past;
Just space to stand once more and taste the wind.

Wittgenstein thought long and hard about the image of time past.
There was no pleasure in it: a grammar of wave and wind.

He studied bad American movies from the front row. The past
Rose like a cathedral's magnified St. Francis preaching to wind-

Stunned birds, yet when *The End* languidly passed,
His eyes blurred in the projector's false light. A wind

Goes through all things and had we eidetic recall the past
Would contain all instants layered in a box. Benjamin's wind

Litters Viennese squares. The time for paradise is past
Time, surely. Only birds ask: *What is time in terms of wind?*

BEYOND BOOK'S HORIZON

AT WALLACE STEVENS' GRAVE

so that each of us
Beholds himself in you, and hears his voice
In yours, master and commiserable man
"To an Old Philosopher in Rome"

Whenever people gesture and their gestures melt in air,
Lightly, for split seconds, then recur in the mind
The way fragments of a jar in Paris revert to wholeness
On their way back up to the ledge or table fallen from,
To be shown in flaky black and white, down and up,
Reassembling and breaking apart on worn flagstones,
Up and down, again and again, for the wonderment
Of those watching the flicker of the first projector,
And sucking in their breath and letting out their breath:
    Our modern frieze

Of the life we have descended from in one unbroken
Line begun with those luminaries now facing us on stamps,
White-suited and bow-tied in chill repose, their brows
Thickened in thought, their hands stilled from invention,
Their angular jaws clenched against the photographer's lens;
Whenever I have stopped to consider the allurement
Proffered by some diver poised on the sudden brink,
Then in cleaving flight, piercing the gray pool water
Whose froth slowly erupts and then fountains slowly back
    Into the pool,

Only to just as slowly reverse course and stream down feet,
Legs, trunk with the now-drying black suit, as the anonymous
Body arcs up and jackknifes back onto the springing board

That slowly settles to rest as he backwards steps off: whenever,
I say, I have stopped half-way myself between stepping off
A corner into traffic, or half-way through revolving doors
In some airport terminus, whenever I have thought of you,
I have thought of those lines of lilting abstractions ascending
And descending through a mind of winter, yours, in all its
    Jar and diver

Stillness and eruption and recovery, and think, too, of
Summer and the Gulf and those long executive weeks
Watching waves curl repeatedly on the hidden sandbar,
Flecking foam soundlessly offshore, while vast stanzas
Of some unwritten poem begin to assemble and dissolve
In vistas of intellect; and it is this image I see whenever
I hear in my ear one of your poems, uncoiling its length,
Or tolling its syllables one after the next, down the page
And up the next, until I cannot fathom any expression of
    Remorse or love,

Peter Quince, nor any landscape or gesture or rhythm
That does not have as its echo one of yours, early or late;
And thus when I picture (always without color or sound)
The hedgerows and tamped gravel walks, the isolate figures
With or without lilies, the gravestones unadorned or adorned
By trumpet or angel or, in Roman style, open scroll with one
Student attending at the side of the seated bearded magus,
I see in my mind's eye the jar even such an age as ours
Surrounds, much as hand surrounds lily, or pool water diver,
    And just this

I know is true and false, one and the same, that your poems
Are a bat of lathes and struts eager to take to air, and you,
An old philosopher in the Rome of the mind, rigging ideas
To astonish clouds, though we sit like the thinker in Picasso's
Fall of Icarus, perplexed, hand clasping hand, watching
The downward sloping path of the one sailing through blue.
If nothing can save us from this gravity, if nothing keeps us
From looking upward and looking downward with longing,
Then we may find solace in art, which, like the vision of Er,
    Rises from death.

FOR Z. HERBERT

Q: You are a pessimist?
A: I don't agree. I am not an optimist either. Rather,
I am a Greek. I believe the Golden Age was long ago.

I would choose a glittering plain
Though here is no plain
Or an agora with greybeard thinkers
Though the colonnade's deserted

I would choose a symposium
Though guests never come
Or a stout ship bound for spice
Though shipwrights have set sail

I would choose a mountain
One impossible peak
Though it's dull earth for leagues
A little breeze wafts a feather

I would choose heroic staves
Something noble something hard
Durable like armor on Argives
Something a lame songmaker

Bad in one eye
Could yet fashion from memory
Stitching one verse to the next
A chant of ten thousand spear

See him sitting there in the dirt
Outside his cinderblock hut
Which in his mind's a palace
Many-roomed like Ariadne's

He sits poking a thumb in dust
We are not the dust of a dusty tribe
He scratches out an acropolis
That to the one-eyed might be Troy

His lyre is catgut on a plastic jug
His hands arthritic his lips cracked
His white hair comes out in tufts
His koine an old man's treble

He chants of the forest people
Black bread the hunt for boar
Where no Penelope holds out
Nor ruined prince ransomed back

His hands scrabble in the dirt
A stylus a forefinger's nail
He chants he sways he moans
His is an elegy for the departed

A tower he calls into being
Instead of thunderheaded gods
There is dust and a feather
And a winding stair with treads of salt

POSTHUMOUS

But me they'll lash in hammock, drop me deep.
Fathoms down, fathoms down, how I'll dream fast asleep.
                                    "Billy in the Darbies"

Over gin, I could tell you of the one in Melville's desk;
Or of *Walden*'s author ruefully joking about his attic—
"The largest private library in Massachusetts"—all
His own returned (at cost) from the publisher; or
Of what you have probably already heard of Emily's
Stitched together fascicles stuffed into deal dressers;

Or on and on: the grim reapings, the frayed stained
Manuscripts—shitty sheets, according to Catullus—
Left to wool and dust gather, left to the vagaries
Of the living, with their sad agendas, left here to us
To imagine, as I do this evening, the to-be-hanged
Billy Budd and his death-dreaming conjurer, Herman,

Who himself at the end was unread, inconsolable,
Certain failure would consign to nothingness (gelid
As any Atlantic gravewater) what his pen gleaned
In the hours of night that still called him to write;
And then I picture Severn's last sketch of Keats,
Who coughing blood knew "ambition blind"—

Sure his lungs' fillings and heavings were but prelude
To a stone's *Here lies One Whose Name was writ in Water*
(Discarded drafts crumpled like stained bedclothes).
Yet so marvelous to relate that posterity relinquishes
Even such as these from its unwitting maw, and there
They are in fine dust-jackets, ranged in any bookseller,

Alphabetized and upstanding, a host of the drowned,
Swelling the ranks of the verily great so that tales
Of rejection seem mere Hollywood histrionics,
While the years of acclaim, poetic justice—posthumous,
But no worse for that, no worse. At the end of his life,
O'Neill enjoined Carlotta, his last and best muse,

To seal in wax the typescript of "Long Day's Journey"
—The smeared pages "written in tears and blood"—
And never stage the drama: the groin-kicking Tyrones
Too like his own drunken agon to be granted voice.
I once heard the actor Robards tell of the opening night
In 1955, how the audience at the final curtain rushed

From boxes, stormed down aisles, until they ceased
Applause and stared up at the cast's glistening eyes.
(Yes, Carlotta betrayed O'Neill's behest, and so . . . ?)
I watched Robards, near death himself, recount how
All then stood silently, tasting the playwright's words.
I too smiled as he smiled at that belated triumph.

Over my desk, a portrait of grey-eyed Hopkins:
Behind him the terrible sonnets, before him typhoid;
All my undertakings miscarry, a barren summation;
Buried at Glasnevin—unpublished, unknown.
In decades: counter, original, strange. (Praise him!)
His executor, the laureate Bridges, read no longer.

Tonight the moon journeys to Keats's death mask
Under glass in a Rome museum; to lone foretopmen
Undone by jury; and to our own, the hammock-lashed,
Sunk in the gloom of ruination, and the ache of bone
Held, held in the tightening grip of incomprehension:
Those the future may restore to us, even against their will.

GLOSSARIUM

My suggestion is that we, as glossers and glozers,
approach Vaughn's poems like well-meaning
Pharisees. We may or may not see the light.
Geoffrey Hill, *Style and Faith*

These syllables lost:
no mouth bemoaning
their centuries' sleep
under monastic ruins,
in scrolls lost to time.
Lost, the spellbound
runes of a friar's hand,

headaches for a muzzy
scholar's brain: belated
slantings on vellum.
Crosswings of script
arc beyond book's horizon
to the primal word, un-
said, unheard, yet read.

So pages darken
as sun burns a cloister's
red violent windows where
saints drizzle from clouds.
I grasp threads of riven
conjunctions, nouns gone
from commonrooms,

only to wholly lose
my sense of how words
follow in natural sequence.
From an oak bench,
I watch an eighty-year-old's
brilliantly white head
bow before workbook's

spidery translation.
Daylight now falls
until a lone name-stone,
interlace cross intact,
defines the coming night;
rows of gas lamps glaze
damp stone walls.

As scholarship fades,
a parallax view joins
words and worlds;
shelves of volumes
darken until gone
the way of Passion plays
and hagiographies,

disorders of the pre-
Renaissance (dark, middle,
forgotten) and, hence,
devolve to inchoate lines
warped by ignorance
(sin's other face):
so many inert signs

beyond any semiotics
of saving grace. Thrushes
sing from the outside in,
as if to say the world's
out there, out there. . . .
In stone chambers, what
faith I have in words falls

with the susurrations
of dry leaves dislodged
from spine-broken tomes.
My fingertip roams
over ancient lemmas—
involute explanations
muddle understanding.

Seen thus, the gloss (from
Gr. *tongue* and, by extension,
language) requires its own
diminutive shadow: an
interstice of word
and word forming a self-
reflexive net that shall

cover each page
with spiraling minute
glyphs, thereby triggering
an infinite regress
through leather-backed
blackness into the void
of meaninglessness.

In such labyrinths,
dead reckoning
by the Word's first light
is the only way out:
a resurrection of sorts
as it must have seemed
for cathedral schools

that once sought from
marginal means the straight
path to the stars. William
of Conches' twelfth-century
Glosae super Platonem
plied constellated skies
of the *Timaeus,* seeking

Christian cosmology: an
acrostic balancing act's
two suns overlap and earth's
born twice (though pagan
work is always false).
While fictions shadow forth
truth, the glossing hand

also lies, as Franciscans
early on recognized: the wit
of mendicant preachers
twisting the pure text;
whence the Middle English
glosen signifying both
"explain, interpret,"

but also "obscure truth,
disguise, embellish, gloss
over"—these meanings
fittingly self-eclipsing.
Glossing requires glozing,
the twin sun its other
darker photosphere.

I think of my own youth,
reading above my years,
charmed by Conrad's tone
before I'd tested fear;
the Yeatsian sublime,
Lear's adamantine tears
—hermetic designs

in each turning page.
If youth's a gloss on age,
as Wordsworth thought,
forgetting, willful or not,
acts as memory's gauge;
still, the more I lose,
the more I search in books,

just to uncover this truth:
Age is a gloss on youth.
I step in no book twice
for I'm not the mind I was
even one breath ago.
Here's perhaps one cause:
A trope is a rift in ice,

a fissure explication thaws
when rime's an echoed word.
If we learn by going back
(*Soe soule into the soule may flow*)
we also learn old laws
of entropy and wrack
when memory's disturbed.

Now all is prime
silence among the shelves
and stacks ranged like
important, if dismissed,
centuries, as over beeswaxed
tables the black-suited
librarian hums the time.

Visitors' hours end.
One last shuffling
professor on sabbatical
straightens tie and coat
and glances in sudden
bemusement at the stair's
stark double helix,

an ascension toward what?
rhyme? harmony? or
simply the muffled iteration
of black on white, page
upon page? I shut my eyes
envisioning a celestial
ribbon of marginalia:

a starry threshold
crossed by interlopers
for whom all parallel
lines indeed converge
in the gold-leaf skies
of deep casuistry, as
mind and text merge

on this study table's
fading oblong of quiet:
where shadows spill light
and light shadows dark;
where monks, devout
and aloof, besieged antiquity
for its one ontological

half-truth and in dim
fastnesses across Europe
wrote toward this moment
when their works would rise
through chambered light
to sun's age zero
—word's bloom, lights out.

ENVOI

This book blanched by fire, found in ghetto crawlspace,
has no margin, ink's long since run bleeding word to
word,

smearing, smudging, thumbprint of blood, frayed, torn,
scorched, heel's savage scourge, crumpled, ripped, split in
pain:

were you to hold it up to the ceiling's bare bulb you'd see
the mud, the blood, the butchered blotched rent binding,
page

on page clumped together, smutched idioms sundered:
you'd speak the lines, if you could, from those dark
odes:

learn how their makers were roused, garrisoned, shot,
how their language was unlearned by those who came
after,

how tide upon tide warped letters, crazed and cracked,
whelming their sweet sounds, until all that's left is this
bundle

scarred by torch, by axe, by curse—past blackened door,
past bricked-up casement, in suffocating clouds of bone
ash,

until, gingerly picking your way through the wreckage,
you come at last to claim this alphabet from your still
kingdom.

NOTES

The volume's epigraph is taken from "At Yale," Czeslaw Milosz, *Provinces: Poems 1987–1991,* trans. Czeslaw Milosz and Robert Hass.

Library: The epigraph is translated in the poem's final stanza.

Knowing Greek: Early in the nineteenth century, Lord Elgin brought to Britain large fragments of the Parthenon's monumental frieze. / "Yes, on to Pi . . ." is lifted from Thomas Hardy's "Liddell and Scott, on the Completion of their Lexicon." / "*lads* became *men*": British soldiers' diction grew more prosaic as the war went on (see Paul Fussell's *The Great War and Modern Memory*). / "Even as an event in English history": J. S. Mill, quoted in Richard Jenkyn's *The Victorians and Ancient Greece.* / "Force is any *x* that makes a thing out of a mortal . . ." paraphrases Simone Weil's view (in *The Iliad, Or the Poem of Force,* trans. Mary McCarthy) that "[t]he true hero . . . of the *Iliad* is force. . . . It is that *x* that turns anybody who is subjected to it into a *thing*."

For One Who First Showed Me Scipio's Dream: Scipio's dream-journey through the heavens is described in Cicero's *On the Republic.*

The King's Question: That the King's question is lost is my own invention. In Herodotus, the episode constitutes a striking example of the danger of misinterpreting the oracle's ambiguous answer, as Croesus's question, regarding the advisability of his launching a war, results in the very thing he wished to avoid: his own defeat (*History,* 1:46–86). I have substituted one irony for another. *I count the grains of sand . . .* : I have recast the Pythia's lines from those given by Michael Wood in *The Road to Delphi: The Life and Afterlife of Oracles.*

The Last *Canto*: Arrested in 1945 for treason and detained at Pisa, Pound was held for weeks in an open-air cage, then sent to St Elizabeth's, in Washington D.C., where he remained for many years. Hugh Kenner's *The Pound Era* discusses Pound's preternatural silence following his repatriation to Italy. According to Kenner, "Tempus loquendi, tempus tacendi" ("A time for speaking, a time for keeping silent") was Pound's statement when, at an opera, he was asked by the audience for some words. The last two lines of the poem are lifted from Pound's final, fragmentary *Canto*.

Shadow Work: "Sicilian quarries": in Thucydides' account of the ill-fated Athenian expedition of 413, the survivors, having endured seventy days imprisoned in quarries, were sold into slavery. / I have relied on Michelle P. Brown's *Painted Labyrinth: the World of the Lindisfarne Gospels* for details of the Viking raids on the British monastery.

Philosophy, Writ Small: Italicized sections are lifted from W.G. Sebald's *The Rings of Saturn* (trans. Michael Hulse), in which the narrator ruminates on Sir Thomas Browne's seventeenth-century *Discourse of the Sepulchral Urns lately found in Norfolk* (commonly known as *Urn Burial*). I have taken the liberty of putting Sebald's prose—itself a free adaptation of Browne's words—into stanzaic form.

Angelus Novus: Walter Benjamin's "Theses on the Philosophy of History" glosses Paul Klee's painting, "Angelus Novus." / "Blue Book": the *Blue and Brown Books* Wittgenstein originally dictated to his Cambridge students during the 1933–34 session.

At Wallace Stevens' Grave: The phrase "a bat of lathes and struts" is lifted from Guy Davenport's description of da Vinci's experimental aviation design ("The House That Jack Built" in *The Geography of the Imagination*). To that same source I owe my knowledge of Picasso's mural of Icarus. / "Er": in Plato's *Republic,* Er—a man thought dead on the battlefield—visits the underworld and, revived, describes the afterlife.

To Z. Herbert: The epigraph comes from *Conversation on Writing Poetry: An Interview with Zbigniew Herbert,* conducted by John and Bogdana Carpenter (*The Manhattan Review,* Winter 1984/5).

Posthumous: For "ambition blind," see the sonnet "I cry your mercy—pity—love!—aye, love," likely composed shortly before the poet's death. Keats wrote his own epitaph *("Here Lies One . . ."); *however, friends were responsible for the reference to his "bitterness in heart," also incised on his gravestone, believing his early death hastened by malicious critical reviews. / *All my undertakings miscarry:* Hopkins met disappointment with hard-won reserve, writing to R.W. Dixon: "[t]he only just judge, the only just literary critic, is Christ, who prizes, is proud of, and admires, more than any man, more than the receiver himself can, the gifts of his own making." [Letter June 13, 1878 in *A Hopkins Reader,* ed. John Pick].

Glossarium: For glossing as a vexed hermeneutic enterprise, and for various references to its historical background, I have leaned hard on Robert W. Hanning's "I Shall Finde It In A Maner Glose: Versions of Textual Harassment in Medieval Literature" (*Medieval Texts and Contemporary Readers,* eds. Finke and Shichtman). / "Name-stones" mark graves in some monastic precincts. / The *OED* defines "lemma" as "the heading or theme of a scholium, annotation, or gloss." / "I step in no book twice . . ." performs a Heraclitan turn on Alberto Manguel's *A History of Reading:* "We never return to the same book or even to the same page, because in the varying light we change and the book changes, and our memories grow bright and dim and bright again, and we never know exactly what we learn and forget, and what it is we remember." / "Soe soule into the soule may flow" is lifted from Donne's "The Extasie."

Envoi: Composed in memory of Martin Birnbaum, a Yiddish poet, who emigrated from the Ukraine in 1923 and lived for many years in Manhattan, where he taught the language.

BRIAN CULHANE was born in New York City in 1954, the son of a legendary animator. After graduating from City University of New York (BA) and Columbia University (MFA), he studied epic literature and the history of criticism at the University of Washington (PhD). His poems have appeared in such literary journals as the *Hudson Review,* the *Paris Review,* and the *New Criterion.* He has lectured on American writers for Humanities Washington, and in 2007 he was awarded an Artist Trust/Washington State Arts Commission Fellowship in Literature. He teaches at Lakeside School, and lives in Seattle with his family. In October 2007, the Poetry Foundation (Chicago) honored Culhane with the Emily Dickinson First Book Award, for a poet over fifty who has never published a book of poems. This is his winning collection: *The King's Question.*

This book was designed by Rachel Holscher. It is set in New Baskerville type by BookMobile Design and Publishing Services, and manufactured by Bang Printing on acid-free paper.